Mary Stuart

BY THE SAME AUTHOR

Mary Stuart

A Play by John Drinkwater

Revised Edition

London: Sidgwick & Jackson, Ltd.
3 Adam Street, Adelphi.   1922

First Published, March, 1921
Second Impression, April, 1921
Third Impression, June, 1921
Revised and Reset (Fourth Impression), September, 1922

All Dramatic Rights reserved by the Author

PRINTED IN GREAT BRITAIN BY
BILLING AND SONS, LTD., GUILDFORD AND ESHER

TO

NORA AND ST. JOHN ERVINE

AUTHOR'S NOTE

THIS revised version, published in September, 1922, is, with certain modifications, the original form of the play, from which I departed for reasons that need not here be discussed, and which is the final form in which I wish to leave it.

J. D.

THE CHARACTERS ARE:

Andrew Boyd.

John Hunter.

Mary Stuart.

Mary Beaton.

David Riccio.

Darnley.

Thomas Randolph.

Bothwell.

MARY STUART

ACT I

A small library in ANDREW BOYD'S *house in Edinburgh. In the far wall is a fireplace, and to the
right of it a high folding window. Above the
fireplace is a large oil portrait of Mary Stuart.*

*It is late on a summer evening, and the window is open,
giving on to a garden terrace, under which the town
lies in the moonlight.*

ANDREW BOYD, *who is seventy years old, sits at a small
table with a slight, querulous, but not charmless, young
man,* JOHN HUNTER. BOYD, *wearing a black velvet
coat and skull-cap, looks as Charles the First might
have done had he achieved a fuller age.* HUNTER
is in evening clothes. The date is 1900 *or later.*

Hunter: That's all. It's terrible.

Boyd: What do you propose to do?

Hunter: I don't know. What can I do?

Boyd: Did you merely want to tell me—or do you
want my advice?

Hunter: Andrew, the few grains of wisdom I have
I've picked up from you. At least, I think so.
Help me—if there is any help.

Boyd: I don't know that I can guide your moods.

That's difficult always between men.   I can only try to tell you what I think.   Is it worth while?

Hunter: Well?

Boyd: You and Margaret have been married five years, isn't it?   It's not long, but it's a good deal in young lives.

Hunter: Five years—yes.

Boyd: They have been happy years, haven't they?

Hunter: Perfectly, until this.

Boyd: They seemed so, to you.   And now—by the way, have you ever cared for any other woman?

Hunter: No.

Boyd: No.   And now there's Finlay.   I've always liked Finlay.   And his book on our Queen is the wisest word about her that I know.

Hunter: My God!   It's funny, isn't it?   Finlay on harlotry.   I beg your pardon, Andrew.

Boyd: That's just it, my boy. Harlotry.   The word buzzes in your brain, doesn't it?   I wonder. Do you want to understand at all—or do you just mean to be angry?

Hunter: It's easy enough to understand.

Boyd: No; never easy.   It needs patience, and love.

Hunter: I understand, bitterly, because I love.

Boyd: It needs patience, and love.   And there must be no confusion of pride.

Hunter: What do you mean?

Boyd: There are women whose talent it is to serve.   And some are great lovers.

Hunter: I kept no love from her.

Boyd: Was it enough?

Hunter: What does that mean? I tell you she loves Finlay.

Boyd: How do you know?

Hunter: She told me.

Boyd: It was not a secret that you surprised?

Hunter: No.

Boyd: Have you liked Finlay?

Hunter: I suppose so. Yes—it's the uglier for that.

Boyd: She told you at once?

Hunter: I think so. Yes, I'm sure of that.

Boyd: Do you want her love?

Hunter: That's absurd, Andrew.

Boyd: What is the most precious thing in the world to you? In your emotions?

Hunter: That is. You know.

Boyd: Or your sense of mastery in owning her?

Hunter: You can't refine things like that.

Boyd: But you must, or fall into the mere foolishness of life. You must answer yourself. Do you want to enjoy her love, or do you want to enslave it?

Hunter: How can I believe that what she gives to Finlay isn't taken from me?

Boyd: She can take nothing from you that is yours.

Hunter: Her love belongs to me.

Boyd: If you can keep it.

Hunter: You are an old man, Andrew, and my best friend.

Boyd: Yes, you are angry. You are afraid. You fear for your pride. And there is but one salvation. Perfect love casteth out fear.

Hunter: How could she—how could she? I was so happy always—that at least seemed safe.

Boyd: I was never married, but I have understood women. Or I think so. That's an old man's compliment to himself. Men use them ill.

Hunter: But they can destroy us. Look at this.

Boyd: Yes, I know. They can be wild in the wits, too. But not as you mean. And they have the better excuse, perhaps. I want you to see this, John. It is you that are in peril of sin here, not she.

Hunter: But I have done nothing but love her.

Boyd: You have accused her.

Hunter: She accused herself.

Boyd: Accused?

Hunter: Call it what you will.

Boyd: Let us call it the right thing.

Hunter: Well?

Boyd: She did not accuse herself, I think. She trusted you, splendidly.

Hunter: That's oddly put, isn't it? The trusting, surely, was mine.

Boyd: I think not, not at least as you see it. What was it you trusted?

Hunter: Margaret's devotion.

Boyd: Her love of you, you mean?

Hunter: Yes, that.

Boyd: Has she betrayed your trust?

Hunter: What's the use of saying it over and over again?

Boyd: There's folly in it, my boy, and I want you to see it. I want you to see exactly where the betrayal is, so that whatever you do shall not be done blindly. You trusted Margaret's love. It is a wide thing, radiant, the capacity in her for loving?

Hunter: I was envied—everywhere.

Boyd: Very well. She gave her love to you, freely. I've seen it, and I know its richness. Suppose it had been a poor mean thing, with no roots, subject to little dark intrigues, lightly given and lightly taken away. Then this new interest, or any, would have been—what shall we say—a peccadillo—something to hide, wouldn't it?

Hunter: I don't know. Perhaps. I suppose so.

Boyd: But Margaret is not made for these slight occasions, is she? You know that, or the better man in you knows it. It is the insignificant heart that is furtive, not worth loving. But Margaret hid nothing.

Hunter: I don't understand that part of it. That she told me doesn't help the pity of it—but why did she tell me?

Boyd: I said. Because she loves you, and because she trusted you splendidly.

Hunter: Trusted me in what?

Boyd: To understand. That was beautiful homage to your love. But you cannot understand. She may be learning that now. Perhaps in her heart she knew it before. I wonder.

Hunter: What do you want me to believe?

Boyd (*rising and moving to the portrait of* MARY STUART): She, too, was a great lover. I am an old man, and I have enjoyed many things. Life has been full, life here about me, and the life of history and the poets. And one has been as real as another.

He moves to the open window and looks out.

There in Edinburgh was lived the saddest of all histories, the tragedy of all such women who are unlucky in their men—Margaret's tragedy, perhaps.

Hunter : But your Queen——

Boyd : No, don't be impatient. Mary Stuart is in my blood, I know, but I am thinking of your trouble only, John. Have you ever reflected on the strangeness of that Edinburgh story—the confusion of it, growing and growing through the years? History never so entangled itself. All the witnesses lied, and nearly all who have considered it have been absorbed in confirming this word, refuting that. And at the centre of it, obscured by our argument, is the one glowing reality, a passionate woman. Beside that, the rest is nothing, but we forget.

Hunter : What has this to do with Margaret?

Boyd : It is Margaret. These women—such women—are sometimes destroyed finding no man who can know all that they have to give. Is Margaret to be destroyed? Ask yourself. Such as these do not love unworthily—it is lamentable when they love unworthy men.

Hunter : Is a man unworthy, thinking of his honour?

Boyd : You talk amiss, talking so. History seethes with the error, society is drenched with it. Mary Stuart cared nothing for your honour—nor does Margaret. The lovers are wiser than that.

Hunter : Then I've done with it.

Boyd : No, surely. What is this honour that you extol?

Hunter : My right, my dignity, my manhood.

Boyd: And you have lived with the philosophers and the poets. Verily a little wind against the reason in our own lives—John, boy, your honour is pride, a poor brute jealousy, cruelty. That is the truth. Will you learn it?

Hunter: You know nothing.

Boyd: I know all.

Hunter: She has failed me.

Boyd: Why? Is your wife a light of love?

Hunter: I believed not.

Boyd: You know it. Does she love Finlay finely —as you would be loved?

Hunter: As I——

Boyd: As you would be loved?

Hunter: How can I——

Boyd: No—answer honestly. You know.

Hunter: I tell you she must choose.

Boyd: Be careful—or the choice will destroy you. And it will be of your making, not hers. Remember that.

Hunter: I gave her everything.

Boyd: It was a great gift. And Finlay's is that too, I think. Or was yours but a poor venture, the tribute of a little soul? Is Margaret to have no better luck than that poor Queen? Or can Finlay——? Down there at Holyrood? Look, in the moonlight. A woman of great wit—Margaret is that too. And nothing better coming to her than a scented pimp, a callow fool, and a bully. They should have been three great princes, masters of men. And just that.

A dog howls across the garden below.

It's the moon. But her love was magnificent.

And Margaret's is. A new unhappy queen? I wonder.

Hunter (*rising and moving to* BOYD): Look here, Andrew, you can't alter facts by filming them over with dead romances. I gave Margaret everything, and she wants to give me a part at best—nothing, may be. It's a bad bargain, and I won't make it. Damn that dog.

As it howls again.

Why should I allow Finlay to meddle with my life?

Boyd: Your life is but a part of life. It began, and it will go on in time beyond yourself. You and Margaret and Finlay are a part of life, not of some little local interest of your own. Mary knew it. Do you know her poem? It's here.

He moves to the picture and reads from under it.

> Ill names there are, as Lethington,
>   Moray, Elizabeth;
> By craft of these I am undone,
>   And love is put to death.
>
> Though brighter wit I had than these,
>   Their cunning brought me down;
> But Mary's love-story shall please
>   Better than their renown.
>
> Mary the lover be my tale
>   For the wise men to tell,
> When Moray joins Elizabeth
>   And Lethington in hell.
>
> Not Riccio nor Darnley knew,
>   Nor Bothwell, how to find
> This Mary's best magnificence
>   Of the great lover's mind.

They sing it sometimes in Edinburgh still. How would you like Margaret to make such a song of you? 'This Margaret's magnificence of the great lover's mind.' There's a fellow who sings it some nights down there. And old Andrew Boyd hears it —three hundred years and more afterwards, and he knows the truth of it, as all wise men would. And John Hunter may be forgotten, not like a Mary Stuart, but the thing that John Hunter means will endure, always, and wise men would know the truth of it for ever.

Hunter: Would you madden me? Why?

> *A voice singing is heard away in the night, faintly.*

I would give anything to know that Margaret loves me—there. But, Finlay—what is there in Finlay that she can't find in me?

Boyd: A vast, separate, breathing creation of God. Would you dare to forbid a woman's love of that? You are ambitious.

Hunter: What would she say, do you think, if I loved this woman and that, here and there?

Boyd: She would despise you. Because you think of it lightly, as an easy and deliberate thing. You don't mean love. You mean a trivial, feathery visiting, that does not know what love is. There he is—listen.

> *The voice below becomes articulate as the song ends.*

> Mary the lover be my tale
> For the wise men to tell,
> When Moray joins Elizabeth
> And Lethington in hell.

> Not Riccio nor Darnley knew,
> Nor Bothwell, how to find
> This Mary's best magnificence
> Of the great lover's mind.

Hunter: It's a damned silly song. What's it all about? A dog singing, and a fool joining in, and you chattering against all sense.

He moves back to the table.

Boyd: You are emphatic—the emphasis that knows it is misplaced.

He goes again to the portrait.

Look at this Queen. She had wisdom, the wisdom of love. In that presence you could learn; learn to see your story a little more truly, John. She could tell you of courage, which is all, greater than pride or fear. She does tell you, doesn't she? Doesn't she?

Hunter: What does a dead queen know about me? You talk nonsense. The moon has your wits, you're like the crazy singer out there. Mary Stuart can tell me nothing I say. My God! What's that?

A dress rustles outside on the terrace.

Boyd: What's the matter?

He turns.

Hunter: There—look—— Who is it?

MARY STUART *stands on the terrace at the window. She is the Queen of the portrait.*

Mary: Boy, I can tell you everything.

*   *   *   *   *

BOYD *and* HUNTER *and the portrait and the
moonlit terrace pass into nothingness, and we see*
MARY STUART'S *room in Holyrood on the
evening of March the ninth,* 1566. MARY *is
lying asleep on a couch,* MARY BEATON *seated
beside her, reading. After a few moments the
Queen moves uneasily, and in again a few
moments she wakes.*

Mary: Poor boy—poor boy. If he would but
listen—but how strange. What a thing was that to
dream ? Out there—somewhere in the moonlight—
I listened. Dreams should be of the past, surely.
That's the way of them, isn't it, Beaton ?

Beaton: Of the past—yes—or timeless.

Mary: But this was of some far to-morrow. We
are part of life for ever—we become what we are for
ever. I heard the old man say it. I heard it in my
dream.

Beaton: What was it, madam ?

Mary: How long have I slept ?

Beaton: An hour, hardly.

Mary: I passed down the ages in an hour. It was
in some life when I was an old and argued story.
Generations and generations after us. A boy and
his lover, and Mary Stuart breathing again in a new
sorrow—the sorrow that is eternal.

Beaton: You were restless.

Mary: I was travelling far.

Beaton: Dreams are full of trickery for my part.

Mary: And sometimes they are the heart of us.
How will it be told of me ? I wonder. Not a man
for ever, perhaps, to know the truth of it. But the

old man knew. If it could be known—that should
be good counsel for all foolish lovers, I think. I
know love, that at least. Beaton, the intrigues of
Europe will destroy me—no, they will. But I know
love. If it could be a light to all such poor boys.
Where is Riccio?

Beaton: Shall I find him?

Mary: No; I asked incuriously.

Beaton: He grows more daring.

Mary: He sings well.

Beaton: Is that all, madam?

Mary: Unhappily, with him too. Riccio, Darnley,
Bothwell. You must not breathe a word of Bothwell, Beaton. That must not be known. But they
make a poor, shabby company. Riccio sings, yes,
ravishingly. And no more. Darnley cannot sing even,
and he's my husband. Just a petulance—one cannot
even be sorry for it. How he hates Riccio—I wish
David were better worth hating. That would be
something. And Bothwell wants to take me with
a swagger. It's a good swagger, but that's the end
of it. I think he will take me yet, the odds against
him are pitiful enough. But it's a barren stock of
lovers, Beaton. I, who could have made the greatest
greater.

Beaton: He may come.

Mary: Craft is against me, my friend. I shall
have no leisure to find the great one. Lethington
works, and my brother Moray works. And Elizabeth
waits. Elizabeth of England—they will do as she
wishes. She knows it, and I know. I am too
beautiful for her. She has poets who call her

beautiful, too. If Mary were their Queen, what a song it would be. She knows it. It's a little secret satisfaction that.

Beaton: You match them all, madam, in wits.

Mary: I shall know that till the end. But the end will be to their hand. Fools for lovers, and fools to destroy me. Proudly I shall know that always, being above them in love and wisdom. But love will cheat me, and my wisdom will spare me nothing. That is how it is for me. Riccio is not near?

Beaton (*opening the door*) : No, madam.

Mary: Then listen. This is made for myself, but you shall hear it.

She sings.

Ill names there are, as Lethington,
    Moray, Elizabeth ;
By craft of these I am undone,
    And love is put to death.

Though brighter wit I had than these,
    Their cunning brought me down ;
But Mary's love-story shall please
    Better than their renown.

Mary the lover be my tale
    For the wise men to tell
When Moray joins Elizabeth
    And Lethington in hell.

Not Riccio nor Darnley knew,
    Nor Bothwell, how to find
This Mary's best magnificence
    Of the great lover's mind.

Beaton : It's well done.

Mary : Truly, at least.

Beaton : Your hair ?

Mary : Yes.

Beaton (*arranging it*) : If I were a queen——

Mary : No, Beaton, you wouldn't, I've told you that often enough. The nets are too strong, too well cast. If the Queen's luck is bad, it must be the Queen's luck still. We do not make our choice. The rewards do not consider us. No—the blue pin, so. Hugo Dubois, in an elaborate treatise on the coiffure, says—' women of a fair complexion, coming at night into company, do much affect azure or lazuline gems for the hair, as it were cornflowers in sunny corn ; and to my mind it does well become them.' There—that will do, Beaton.

A knock at the door.

Who is it ?

BEATON *goes to the door and opens it. It is* RICCIO.

Riccio : You are employed, madam ?

Mary : No. Come in, David. Let us be idle. Presently, Beaton.

BEATON *goes.*

Riccio : Idle ? Yes, lady, to receive homage is a business light enough.

Mary : To receive homage lightly given.

Riccio : Yet all queens have found it in their profession, they say. And lightly given? Worthless, if you will, but not that. Not of Riccio, madam.

Mary : You correct me.

Riccio : I know you as you do not yourself.

Mary : This Holyrood is a grey place. A little phrase will tell.

Riccio : It is the chosen palace of the world.

Mary : Yes, your gallantry has an echo, David, a dear one.

Riccio : Let it be that. I will serve even so.

Mary : France—it is a word that I think will become surfeiting in time, it is so beautiful. France. Too sweet, men will say, lilies too often sung, and stale. But how precious it is. They can love there.

Riccio : We are of the south.

Mary : Yes, you have a good suit there.

Riccio : If you would but listen.

Mary : I listen, daily.

Riccio : I do not persuade well.

Mary : You spare nothing.

Riccio : I am suspect in the palace, more and more. Your lord, the King, chiefly.

Mary : Do you stay in Scotland for popularity? They do not choose your kind, David.

Riccio : Every mile of it is abominable. But I stay, eagerly.

Mary : Why?

Riccio : It is adorable of you to answer so yourself.

Mary : Your wit survives.

Riccio : But you shall not steal my pleasure. You ask, to hear me say it. Yes—I beg—it is so! I stay because the compass moves with you. The south has all the enchantments of the heart, there are the spices and the music. I can breathe only there, life is valuable only in that zone of supreme devotions. And where you are, is the south. That is why I stay. It's the answer you foresaw?

Mary: Riccio, with so many advantages. And yet—man, could I but speak for you.

Riccio: I need no ambassadors, madam.

Mary: But you do, Riccio. I could prompt you—but, no.

Riccio: My phrases lack—ah, they grow rusty in these damp airs.

Mary: The phrases are well enough. They would pass in the most elegant of courts, David. Or you should take them to my sister, Elizabeth. She collects them—half the poets of England send her mottoes in this kind. They know better, but it humours her. I myself can match them, excel them, Pierre Ronsard tells me. But what have these to do with me? I have a husband.

Riccio: A husband——?

Mary: And he is nothing. I should, being Mary Stuart, forget him, but he hangs about the place. And I say that to you, David, to you, licensed with the graces of my lovely France, and with some favours in your remembrance, eh? And what do you answer?

Riccio: Answer?

Mary: God, man, yes, answer.

Riccio: If my lord the King fails, may not I——

Mary: Console my—exile?

Riccio: It is allowed.

Mary : A justifiable intrigue ? Commendable, even ?

Riccio : You know it, madam.

Mary : And what is your device for the occasion, David ?

Riccio : To tell you this—always and always— you are the queen of all beauty, the adorable fragrance of——

Mary : No better than that. You lamentable steward.

Riccio (*taking her hand*): I love you, Mary.

Mary (*moving from him*) : And you can say that, and make it no better than an impertinence.

Riccio : I love you—I will take you—so.

Mary : You have not the stature, my poor David. Listen. I meant no anger. Sing to me, often. Your songs come out of a cherished life. Flatter me some- times if you will—I am queen enough to thank my courtiers—and they do not much breed them here in Scotland. And your manners adorn ceremony always —I do not undervalue that—the example is needed. I must not lose you, David, I take pleasure in your company, in your amiability—it is not common. And be content—you will find in this all necessary satis- faction—I shall not starve your nature. But it will be well for us not to speak again of love.

Riccio : To be forbidden that——

Mary : It will be an agreeable distress, never fear. And perhaps in some fortunate, some—unaccus- tomed moment of understanding, you may make a song of me. If it should be so, remember this— you will make little enough of it now, but, then, remember it, if you would make the song well. Mary Stuart was a queen of love, but she had no subjects. She was love's servant, but she found no lord. That is all.

Riccio : No subjects. It is cruel to say that—you know.

Mary : No subjects. Only strangers at the table.

Riccio : I do not understand you, Mary.

Mary : You have said it.

Riccio : I give you myself—all my poet's heart. Is it not enough?

Mary : You are neither subject nor lord. There is no peace in you, David. Just a buzzing in the jar.

Riccio : There are men whose pride you should learn for less than this.

Mary : Ah, then.

Riccio : But my devotion will stay.

Mary : It will satisfy you. It is all that matters. And I am grateful. You are a good secretary, David.

Riccio : What is the love you look for?

Mary : Rest from tumult. Escape. You could not know.

Riccio : No. But I pity you.

Mary : I should reprove you for that. But it's a good venture, the best you could make. It might trouble you. But it will pass. You will think only of yourself to console; that will be your safety.

Riccio : You will not let them dismiss me? I am happy here.

Mary : It is right that you should be happy.   You shall stay, never fear.

Riccio: To serve you always.   I can give light and air a little, that at least.   I should have been king in this place.

Mary (*giving him her hand to kiss*) : Now you may sing to me.

Riccio (*singing*) :

> The snows come, and frosty pools
> > Forbid the birds to sing.
> The pilgrim of the wilderness
> > Complains the tardy spring.
>
> One sits at home in winter ease,
> > And one goes out to find
> In thought of one, the third who waits,
> > But bitterness of mind.

As he sings, DARNLEY *comes in unseen.   He sits, at the far side of the room, listening.*

> Who plays with love, beats up and down
> > The snow beyond the gate.
> Who plays with love is like to tell
> > A spring for ever late.
>
> But this I say, if Holyrood
> > Had crowned a proper king,
> These grey walls had the blossoms worn
> > Of an eternal spring.

Darnley (*not moving—after a silence*) : King David, for example?

Riccio (*rising*) : Sire—we did not know—it was just a rhyme.

Darnley (*rising*) : We did not know—we did not know——

Riccio : Not that—I mean—you startled me.

Darnley : David Riccio—you think I'm a fool.

Riccio : Sire——

Darnley : Well—I'm not.   It's a mistake to think it.   I could make rhymes like that by the bushel if they were worth it.   It's a very ugly song, that.

Mary : It was nothing, my lord.   A tune for idleness.

Darnley : I am instructed.

Riccio : Shall I make such a one for the King ?

Darnley : As this was for the Queen ?

Riccio : If I have not offended.   Would it be Your Grace's pleasure ?

Darnley : There may not be time.

Riccio : Time ?

Darnley : Yes, you know, by the clock.   It passes.   Tick, tick, tick, tick—and you never know.   A rhyme, for instance.   You get one line, and then two, and another, and the end may come, suddenly.   In king's palaces, that is.   Who knows ?

Riccio (*afraid*) : We minstrels delight in parables. You speak in a fine figure, my lord.   But—you do not mean that my poor song has angered you ?

Darnley : A thought only for your next.   A suggestion.   The poet, and time, passing, tick, tick, tick, and the rhyme on the lips, and then—as you will.   I give it you—it may help invention.

Riccio : And—it means nothing more ?

Mary : Come, David, how should it ? (*Directly to him.*) Poets are men, I hope.

Riccio : Surely, madam. I will work upon it, sire. A sonnet, perhaps—no, a ballade—and yet, for the lute——

Darnley : Consider it. (*Going to the door.*) There is a moon. It helps, I am told.

He signs for RICCIO *to go.*

Riccio : Your Grace, I am sure, would not misjudge me.

Darnley : No.

(RICCIO *goes.*)

Mary : What is it ?

Darnley : Shamelessly—so.

Mary : What do you mean ?

Darnley : Always at your ear.

Mary : Well ?

Darnley : What has he been saying to you ?

Mary : It would be tedious.

Darnley : What is he, this fellow ? Your lover ?

Mary : What then ?

Darnley : Am I King of Scotland ?

Mary : Have you—forgotten ?

Darnley : Is he your lover ?

Mary : If he were ?

Darnley : Am I to be common gossip in Edinburgh ?

Mary : Is that all ? No; he is not my lover.

Darnley : They talk. The Queen, they say, has a sweet instructor.

Mary : I have need of such.

Darnley : What is the instruction ?

Mary : Ask your gossips. The word is not mine.

Darnley : Will you dismiss this man ?

Mary : But why should I ? He is a competent secretary. He sings prettily. He has a grace. Why should I lose him ?

Darnley : Because I ask it.

Mary : But I do not remember you.

Darnley : What wit is that ?

Mary : You speak as one privileged to control my affections. I do not remember such a one.

Darnley : This man governs you.

Mary : Alas, no.

Darnley : He guides your policy. The courts of Europe begin to talk of it.

Mary : Poor David. He just sits at the table, and writes as I tell him. There's more policy in a carter.

Darnley : And he is not your lover ?

Mary : No.

Darnley : Then he would be little to lose.

Mary : And yet why should I lose even so little ?

Darnley : I do not believe you.

Mary : So ? And then ?

Darnley : You choose strangely.

Mary : I chose you. God help me.

Darnley : That's ugly.

Mary : What would you have ?

Darnley : What is it to be ?

Mary : How ?

Darnley : I have some rights still, at least.

Mary : You are called king.

Darnley : Then my word should mean something.

Mary : For what ?

Darnley : Dismiss Riccio.

Mary : No.

Darnley : Be careful.   We are not in France.

Mary : You destroy yourself very thoroughly,
Darnley.

Darnley : Dismiss him—or I'll have it sung in
every tavern in Edinburgh.   Or worse.

Mary : Do you love me?

Darnley : What—how do you mean ?

Mary : That's plain enough, man, isn't it ?

Darnley : I have my pride.

Mary : And what of mine ?   I'm hungry—do you
understand ?   All this—my body, and my imagina-
tion.   Hungry for peace—for the man who can
establish my heart.   What do they say—a light
lover, unsure always.   And who is there to make me
sure ?   What man is there with authority ?   Where
is he who shall measure me ?   Listen, my husband.
There are tides in me as fierce as any that have
troubled women.   And they are restless, always,
always.   Do you think I desire that ?   Do you
think that I have no other longings—to govern with
a clear brain, to learn my people, to prove myself
against these foreign jealousies, to see strong children
about me, to play with an easy festival mind, to
walk the evenings at peace ?   Do you think I choose
this hungry grief of passion—deal in it like a little
poet ?   All should be resolved and clear in me, with
a king to match my kingdom.   My love is crazed, a
turbulence, without direction.   It was made to move

3

in long, deep assurance, moulding me beyond my knowledge. I, who should be love, may but burn and burn with the love that I am not. Where is my prophet? Everywhere blind eyes. I took you, I wedded you, I made you king. And you mince, and gossip, and listen at the door. I could have taught you the finest husbandry that Scotland has ever known. And your soul's policy brings you to this. Your craft—the craft of Scotland's excellence —against the poor half-wit of David Riccio. And you have your pride.

Darnley : That at least. For me the rest is past.

Mary : It has never been.

Darnley : No matter—my pride is my pride I tell you. Riccio goes, one way or another. I know my own will—you can't preach me out of that.

At the window.

Look at them, virtuous men and bad men, priests and wenches, liars and gospel, game and the hunters—but all of them with a streak of beastliness in them for the relish of a bawdy tale. And they shall have it. A wallet full of jingles can be bought for a few pence, or I have a turn myself :

> Who's in the Queen's chamber?
> Master Italian Thrift.
> What's the Queen wearing?
> Her long hair and her shift.

Mary : And where's the King of Scotland
> To strike us as we sing?
> And where's the King of Scotland?
> There is no King.

Darnley : I won't have it—do you hear me ?

Mary : I do.

Darnley : Again, will you dismiss Riccio ?

Mary : Must I again ?   No.

Darnley : Then it is your reckoning.   We'll spare you the bawdy songs, perhaps.

Mary : I should.

Darnley : But watch your David—watch him, I say. Keep him close.   That's generous of me—to warn you.   Perhaps now—this minute, or to-morrow, or to-night.   Suspect every footstep.   But I tread lightly. A poor king, but a light step—thus—do you see ?

He creeps to his words towards the door.

Thus—thus—thus—there's a queen in there, and her lover—a dirty lover—thus we go, and thus—be very watchful, madam, very—do you hear them, the queen and her dirty lover—that tongue should be stilled—it isn't decent, is it ?   Then thus, and thus— a light, light tread, eh ?—and thus—ssh !

He goes out.

Mary, *watching him go, laughs, but then with misgiving.   She rings a bell, and* Mary Beaton *comes.*

Beaton : Yes, madam ?

Mary : Did you see anything—out there ?

Beaton : I saw the King pass down the stairs.

Mary : Did he speak ?

Beaton : I don't think he saw me.   He walked oddly—on tip-toe, as though something were at the corner.   And as he went out of sight he half-turned, and put his finger to his lip, and said, ' ssh !' very quietly, like that.

Mary: He's a poor thing, very inconsiderable. But it may happen.

Beaton: What, madam?

Mary: He threatens Riccio.

Beaton: Cannot you satisfy him?

Mary: No. But I have no wish to.

Beaton: We must warn Riccio.

Mary: It would be useless. No, David must take his chance. He knows that there's danger. It's wrong, though, that so slight a man as Darnley should be able to hurt me even so much. Riccio's no matter, really. But if my lord touches him he shall pay as though Riccio were all. Where is Riccio?

Beaton: He was in the yard there, looking out over the town, scraping moss from the wall with his finger. He seemed nervous, I thought.

Mary: That would be monstrous—to have such a man made into a great stake. But it may be.

DARNLEY *is heard singing below the window*

> Who's in the Queen's chamber?
> Master Italian Thrift.
> What's the Queen wearing?
> Her long hair and her shift.

Mary: That's the King of Scotland.

Beaton: Why not send Riccio away? Why let him be, as you say, a great stake?

Mary: Because there is no other. Because my mind is lost, Beaton. Darnley, Riccio, Bothwell— there's a theme for a great heart to play. And there's so much to do. I have talent—as rare as any in Europe. It should be my broad road—that and

my love. And I cannot use it, for my love is beaten
up like dust, blinding me. Wanton, it is said. No
woman I think was ever so little wanton. To be
troubled always in desires—that's to be cursed, not
wanton. Little frustrations, and it should be the
wide and ample movement of life. I want to forget
it all—wholly to become it. And there are Darnley,
Riccio, Bothwell. And my power lies unused, it
rusts. If I could find peace, if there were but a man
to match me, my power should work. Elizabeth
should see an example in Scotland. I would defend
queenship, and I am brought to defend a poor Italian
clerk.

Beaton : Why consider him, or any one of them ?

Mary : It's a madness, isn't it ? But that's the
way. Love is that. We must become love, or it
spends us. I am not Mary Stuart—she is a dream
unspelt. I am nothing. There should have been a
queen, and I am nothing.

RICCIO *comes in, scared.*

Riccio : Madam, forgive me. I don't know what
he means—my lord, the King—he came up to me,
and peered into my face, strangely, and tapped me
on the shoulder, and said—'thieves have irons, and
the crow comes, and the south's as cold as the east.'
He means me harm.

Mary : Come, David, men should have sudden
minds. Calamity is with fortune. Courage, friend.

Riccio : He came to me from below. He's wan-
dering about like a silly ghost. He went back.

He moves to the window—before he gets there,
DARNLEY *is heard again.*

> Who's in the Queen's chamber?
> Master Italian Thrift.
> What's the Queen wearing?
> Her long hair and her shift.

Riccio: What's that? Why does he sing that, under the window?

Mary: It's a brave house for a queen, Beaton, isn't it?

Darnley (*from below*): There's more yet.

> *He sings again.*

> Is there a scullion greedy
> For a crown and a queen's kiss . . .

Mary (*opening window*): Go. Go—I tell you.

> *She closes the window or slams it. Imprecations from* DARNLEY *are heard in the yard below, and a window pane is broken.*

Darnley: Curse you — you harlot — you shall see——

> *His voice fades away.*

Mary: The daughter of France. Pupil of Ronsard. Queen of Scotland.

> DARNLEY *rushes in.*

Darnley: Do you think I will be used so—not by any queen in Christendom.

Mary: Do we talk of using?

Darnley: Do you call me stock? A thing for japes—to be mocked at by a harlot and her creeping filth?

Mary: So, we sing our bawdry at the Queen's window? Where is the King to whip such fellows?

Darnley: We know the window from another.

Mary : Where is the King, I say ?

Darnley : Looking to his own. David Riccio, I spoke too gently in the yard now. Thieves are honest men—but there are rascals, Italian spawn, creeping things—and heels.

Beaton : My lord, this is the Queen's chamber.

Darnley : Ay, the Queen's chamber—that's it. There are heels, I say—and until then, so——

He spits in RICCIO'S *face, and rushes out.*

Riccio (*moving across to* MARY, *and kneeling to her*): He's mad, he should be held. What shall I do, madam ?

Mary : What shall the Queen do ?

Riccio : I am afraid.

Mary : Afraid of that ?

Riccio : They hate me here. He has fellows. It will not be safe for me anywhere in Holyrood. Let me go back to France—Your Majesty can contrive it. I must go.

Mary : Leave us now for a little.

RICCIO *rises and hesitates.*

Go. Stay in your room. You shall not be forgotten. Go, I say.

RICCIO *goes, lamentably.*

Beaton : Madam, madam.

Mary : The measuring is bad, bad. There are matters that the mind must leave. Could you find my Lord Bothwell, do you think ?

Beaton : I will try.

Mary : If you will. Or stay—send Randolph first. Ask him to come here. When he goes, find Bothwell if you can.

Beaton goes. Mary unlocks a cabinet, and takes out a picture of Elizabeth in a jewelled frame, and a paper. The picture she places conspicuously on the top of the cabinet, the paper on the table. Then from the cabinet she takes a small green cloth case, which also she places on the table. She locks the cabinet, and stands on the far side from the door. Beaton returns.

Beaton: Sir Thomas Randolph is here, madam.

Mary: We will receive him.

Beaton moves to the door, and Sir Thomas Randolph, Elizabeth's Ambassador at Holyrood, comes in. Beaton goes. Randolph kneels to Mary, who gives him her hand. He rises, Mary points him to a chair. They both sit.

Mary: Have you more news of our cousin?

Randolph: Her Majesty's physician reports complete recovery.

Mary: You comfort me. Even so slight an indisposition is watched by the world with anxiety.

Randolph: I sent special word to my mistress of Your Majesty's concern.

Mary: I count you always among my true friends. That is to be in a small band, Sir Thomas.

Randolph: I am very sensible of the honour, madam.

Mary: My cousin and I should meet. Such affection should not suffer so long a delay.

Randolph: Her Majesty, I know, is of a like mind.

Mary: If I could but leave this turbulent court

for a time. But, alas, I may not. Can we not persuade the Queen to grace our rough life, think you? She is well served. With such counsellors she could leave with an easy heart. The throne of England knows no insecurities.

Randolph: Her Majesty talks of it often.

Mary: Do you think she will so favour us?

Randolph: I am sure of her inclinations.

Mary: And yet, perhaps, not quite sure.

Randolph: Madam?

Mary: Randolph, I am a woman beset by fools and rascals. Do with that as you will. If I could meet my cousin of England, word to word, she might learn much.

Randolph: She desires that.

Mary: I wonder. To learn might mean admissions. And admissions are dangerous, are they not, even royal admissions?

Randolph: Your Majesty speaks by figures.

Mary: No; plainly. You have your poets. They should tell you what a figure is. But I speak plainly.

Randolph: And yet, madam, not plainly for so plain a man.

Mary: Ambassador from the Court of England? No, Randolph. Elizabeth sends no poor brains on her business. Though I have heard that her wages do not always measure the service.

Randolph: Madam——

Mary: There, there—it's no treason to hear. And I am not a subject of England—yet.

Randolph: A subject?

Mary: One might be a subject of England, or one might be Queen of England—eh, Randolph?

Randolph: Your Majesty can instruct me.

Mary: A subject—or no, that's unlikely; a forfeit rather. Or Queen. Is it not so?

Randolph: How could I say, madam?

Mary: Does not Elizabeth say it?

Randolph: Elizabeth?

Mary: Yes, man. Does she not say it?

Randolph: I cannot say that I have heard Her Majesty——

Mary: Come, Randolph, you are not uninformed. Does she not say it, and fear it?

Randolph: You insist above my knowledge, madam.

Mary: Then answer this, as an honest man. If I leave my kingdom here to its dangers for such time as it may need to travel into England, will the Queen welcome me—receive me even?

Randolph: I can hardly answer that, madam, here.

Mary: Do it by messenger, Sir Thomas, and say no. Not—the Queen's high majesty laments that these present dispositions of her realm—and so forth, in some Cecilian strain, but, bluntly, no.

Randolph: You speak hardly.

Mary: I defend myself. That is all. Though defence is nothing. You might let our cousin know, in some lighter moment, perhaps, that Mary Stuart thought thus—that if she could have found peace and not have been destroyed by base and little lovers, she would have met and instructed the surest wits of England, and have delighted in the match; but that, being tired, she said it was no matter.

Enough, then, but this. Cunning has no pleasure when the heart is breaking. If I ask my cousin to appoint a day, she will not do it.

Randolph: If I might advance the matter as I can——

Mary: Oh, be simple about it, Randolph. Forget your diplomacy—I'm not worth it. Moreover, fate has touched me, and I have a discovering vision. Your genius, my poor Ambassador, fades in the climate of my grief. Policy shines when it is pitted against interest. But my interest knows the doom that is coming. Let us talk as friends, with death appointed. I shall not betray you.

Randolph: Madam, I have my allegiance. But all that devotion may offer is yours. And you speak too hopelessly.

Mary: No. Hope I have mastered—that at least. I shall not want courage, and it may be years. And I shall make a good end. That is all.

Randolph: If some affairs could but be composed, the Queen, I am sure, has good will to you and Scotland.

Mary: To Scotland—where is Scotland, which faction is to be called Scotland? And for me, I tell you, no. Her hope is my destruction; you know it. If I stand before Europe in honour, how long can my cousin delay naming me to her succession?

Randolph: It is her daily dread.

Mary: Dread?

Randolph: Anxiety.

Mary: Dread will do. She fears a Catholic invasion of her throne. That's as may be, but she

fears it. My nomination would foster it, she says
so herself, daily, in dread. My discrediting would
be fortunate. She must be hungry for any word
against me—that could be used. There would be
royal thanks—if no more—for news of Mary Stuart's
offending. Could she be shown, as a wanton, let us
say; or, better, would she but provoke my Lord
Darnley to some violence—what possibilities were
in that. What nets.

Randolph : It is grievous that you should think so.

Mary : Think? Are there not letters? Secrets
that miscarry? Messages that are overheard?
England has her eyes, who knows at what keyhole,
and we must profit by example. Even I have those
about me who are diligent.

She unfolds the paper on the table.

'To His Grace, my Lord of Leicester, from
Sir Thomas Randolph, Ambassador at Holyrood
from the Court of England. My Lord, I learn that
the quarrel between Her Majesty and the King
grows. He of whom I told your Lordship has many
marks of her favour, which the King has been heard
to say do much discredit him to be so slighted for
an Italian jay. So far that much is intended, as I
think, against the intruder, even to extremity, which
indeed may also glance at majesty itself, and so
strike, as it were, to the root. Or if that be not so,
and Master David only be practised against, then
the Queen's anger must be such as will not easily be
paid, and all that is hoped for may be between her
and the King. I am, my Lord, your Lordship's
humble servant, Thomas Randolph.'

Randolph: Madam, I have but to convey what falls out. I set it down, merely. I desire nothing.

Mary: 'All that is hoped for.'

Randolph: By some.

Mary: By my cousin. But we needed no letters. It shall not be kept against you.

She gives him the letter.

And I have a mind that will care for no reckoning—you need not fear. You do but set it down. But I wished you to know. I shall lose, but I know what moves in the dark. There are no surprises, be sure of that.

Randolph: Is there anything that Your Majesty would have me do?

Mary: Be a little sorry for your office, that is all. And remember me as I might have been. You know.

Randolph: You should have been fortunate, madam. You would have borne it greatly.

Mary: You are right about Darnley. He sings bawdy songs at my window.

Randolph: That is lamentable.

Mary: No, it is part of the story. You might have heard him half an hour since. But do not believe all that you hear. David Riccio is nothing. I protect him, as I would my spaniel. But he will serve England's purpose well enough. Let it be. You play your recorder still?

Randolph: Yes, but indifferently.

Mary: Well, I thought, when I heard you. Here is a precious one, of very mellow tone.

She takes it from its case.

It belonged to our French poet, Pierre Ronsard.

Keep it for my sake.   I ask nothing in return.   There is nothing you can do.   Ronsard was a chivalrous poet.   I would have you keep it.

Randolph: It shall instruct me, madam.

> *They rise, and he kneels as she again gives him her hand.*

Mary: Adieu.

Randolph: Madam.

> *He goes.*

> MARY *moves to an open Prayer-Book and turns the leaves.*

Mary (*reading, very quietly, to herself*): 'And in the evening they will return: grin like a dog, and will go about the city. . . .   Unto thee, O my strength, will I sing: for thou, O God, art my refuge, and my merciful God.'

> *She stands silent for a moment.   Then rings the bell beside her.*   BEATON *comes.*

Mary: Did you find my Lord Bothwell?

Beaton: He waits your word.

Mary: Ask him to come.   First draw the curtains and light the candle.

> BEATON *does so, while* MARY *reads again the same passage aloud.*

'And in the evening they will return: grin like a dog, and will go about the city. . . .   Unto thee, O my strength, will I sing: for thou, O God, art my refuge, and my merciful God.'

> BEATON *goes, and* MARY *closes the book.   She stands at the desk, her back to the door.*   BOTH-WELL *appears.*

Bothwell : Madam.

Mary (*half turning*) : My lord.

Bothwell : You sent for me.

Mary : You were not seen to come ?

Bothwell : No.   Not that I care for all their eyes.

Mary : But you must.   I have small reason to cherish security I know; that is past.   But this would confuse things too much.   They will destroy me, but I will not help them too generously.   So this must not be known.

Bothwell : I understand.

Mary : Will you help me ?

Bothwell : Madam, I have no interest but to please myself.   To please you is that.

Mary : Darnley threatens Riccio.

Bothwell : Shall I trip Darnley ?   But why should one be concerned for Riccio ?   There should be better ambitions.

Mary : They think he's my lover.   Or Darnley occupies his mind in a pretence that he thinks it. Let him think it—it is no matter.

Bothwell : Surely not Riccio ?

Mary : No.   But I did not send for you to question me.   Riccio has served me well enough in his kind. I remember these things.   He is in danger, and he must be saved.   That is all.

Bothwell : What can I do ?

Mary : He must leave Scotland, secretly, and at once.   Can you contrive that ?

Bothwell : It could be done.   There is a Dane in port now.   I will give word to the captain.   I have his service.   Tell Riccio to meet me at midnight, by

Frobisher's Croft. I will have a fellow to take him out from shore. When they are clear they can carry a light, and the Dane shall take him up. He can make his own way from Copenhagen?

Mary: Surely. Riccio shall be there at midnight. And my thanks.

She offers her hand.

Bothwell (*taking it*): No more?

Mary: It must not be. No—not yet.

Bothwell: Woman, why do you waste yourself among crowns and peddlers? Who is Elizabeth— who Darnley? What is Scotland, a black country, barren, that it should consume this beauty? You were born to love, to mate strongly, to challenge passion—this passion, I tell you, this. They come to you, and plead as peevish boys, or watch round corners—winds that cannot stir one tress of that hair. You are not aware of them, you are unmoved. But I am not as these—do you think I will wait and wait? I do not plead. I bid your love to me. Mary. Mary. You know it, you know.

Mary: Don't. Think.

Bothwell: But I have thought, and it is enough. You may desert all, but not this.

Mary: Listen. You woo well—boldly at least. Better than Darnley ever did, and Riccio has no more than a little elegance. And he whines. So did Darnley. But you have courage. You are aflame, and I kindle—yes, I tell you so much. What then? Should we leave Scotland? No. Queens are limed. And here, what is there for us but stealthy moments, fugitive? I should burn to them, but they would

but add more smother to my life. I do not know
what may come—I love you, yes, if you will—but no
hope is in it, none. For I must tell you. I am of
those who must be loved always, for all things, for
there to be any peace in love. If you, or any man,
could fathom that—ah, then. You love me now, you
love my beauty. It needs love, it cherishes your love,
it sings back to your hot words. But my beauty is
not all. It will pass, and I should be unsatisfied.
For you could not love me always, for all things.
There is nothing between us but the minute. You
could give me that, but you have nothing else to
give.

Bothwell: And then? Shall the minute be
denied?

Mary: That's good. You make no pretence, even.
But remember, there is no hope in it, there can be
none. Even were Darnley less husband than he is,
and I free to take you to the throne, there would
still be but the minute between us. You are not
the man. He will not come.

Bothwell: I am no schemer in my love. Policy's
a game—there I'm all wits. But love comes, and
is now. You are beautiful, Mary. You betray no
one. What remorse can there be?

Mary: Remorse? No; love is remorseless. But
frustration always, always.

Bothwell: Not of our minute—not of that, I say.

Mary: No, then, not of that.

> BOTHWELL *takes her in his arms, she giving
> herself passionately. After a moment they part,
> as* MARY BEATON'S *voice is heard.*

Beaton (calling from without) : Madam—madam.

Mary : Yes, what is it?

Beaton : Madam.

Mary : Yes, yes—come in.

Beaton (entering) : Madam, the King is crossing the yard—he may be coming here.

Mary (to BOTHWELL) : You must go.

Bothwell : Why should we slink about for any king?

Mary : No — you must. There are confusions enough.

She looks out from the window.

Yes, he is coming. Go through the Close—quickly. At midnight, remember.

BOTHWELL *kisses her hand and goes.*

Beaton : You play very dangerously, madam.

Mary : Beaton, love should be lucky for you. I think it will. But for me . . . He took me in his arms—a moment's fury—fire to slake fire, and that is all. That is my most of love. Why should I not be dangerous?

Beaton : Do you love my Lord Bothwell?

Mary : A little of me—a moment. There is so much else to deny myself, after all. But he means so little more than the others. Still, a little—it is something.

DARNLEY *comes in.*

Darnley : Where has he gone?

Mary : Who?

Darnley : Who? The Italian.

Mary : He is in his room, I think.

Darnley : I saw him go down the far stair as I came in from the yard.

Mary : You are mistaken, I think. Beaton, will you see?

BEATON *goes out.*

Darnley : You know his movements well. But someone went down.

Mary : You are curious.

Darnley : Yes, madam. I must watch these fellows.

Mary : Fellows?

Darnley : Who knows—one, and another perhaps.

BEATON *returns.*

Beaton : Riccio is in his room, madam.

BEATON *goes.*

Darnley : Then, who was it?

Mary : Have you any purpose in coming?

Darnley : Who was it?

Mary : A shadow, perhaps.

Darnley : By God!

Mary : The King then.

Darnley : The King—what king? Who was it?

Mary : You are tiresome.

Darnley : Very well then—look to it that Riccio's matter is not all.

Mary : Riccio's matter?

Darnley : The settlement with him.

Mary : Why did you come? It was not to see a shadow, or a king, or a fellow, or what you will?

Darnley : I came as a friend to warn you. About treason. Do not shelter it. Lest harm coming to it should soil you, too.

Mary : Treason, sir? You speak to the Queen.

Darnley : To be sure, yes. I forgot. I thought it

was to one who played with the Queen's paramour.
I thought I would warn her. I grow forgetful—I
am so busy. A little scheme I have in hand about
the Queen's honour. That's you. Yes. In two
days, or three, or before, perhaps. Pardon me,
madam, I should not intrude in the Queen's
chamber—one never knows who may be in it. That
shadow, now; I wonder. I must investigate—it might
mean another scheme. Once you begin . . . I have
a better tune for the song now—but another time,
another time. But I would not shelter it.

> *He goes.* MARY *takes Elizabeth's picture,*
> *looks at it in the candle-light, and replaces it*
> *in the cabinet, then rings the bell.* BEATON
> *comes in.*

Mary: We will have supper here to-night. Tell
them, will you? And ask Riccio to come. Come
in when you have told them below, and prepare the
table.

Beaton : Yes, madam.

> *She goes.* MARY *takes a purse from the*
> *cabinet, sits, writing a letter, and a moment later*
> RICCIO *comes in.*

Riccio: Madam, the King was here again?

Mary: It's ill-named for him, but he was.

Riccio: I saw him on the green from my window.
He was with my Lord Ruthven and two or three
others, talking. I am afraid. What shall I do?

Mary: All is arranged. You are to meet the Lord
Bothwell by Frobisher's Croft at midnight. A boat
will be ready, and you will wait out at sea till a
Danish ship takes you up. From Copenhagen you

must make your own way to France. Here is money, and a letter to be delivered to Monsieur Carmé in Paris. He will help you if you need it.

Riccio (*taking the purse and letter*): Thank you, madam. If I could but serve you better. But fate is against me.

Mary: Yes, my poor Riccio, fate is against you.

Riccio: I fear for you in this place. There's wickedness in it. If I were but happier in my fate —to shield you.

Mary: You must not let that trouble you. You have done what you could. We are but ourselves. Keep this.

> *She gives him a brooch from her sleeve. He takes it and kisses her hand.* BEATON *comes in.*

Mary: And now we can talk as friends, with no misgiving.

> *She goes to the door and turns the key.*

Beaton, David leaves us to-night. A friendly sail to Denmark has relieved us of our anxieties.

> BEATON *puts wine, cups, and fruit on the table. They seat themselves. They eat and* MARY *pours out the wine.*

Riccio: If you were but coming to France, madam. In a month, how the glades will shine.

Mary: I have them in my mind. Though there are times when one lives too fiercely for the mind's landscapes to be clear. They come in tranquillity. Let us drink to France, the south, where the sun is.

> *They drink.*

Riccio : And to the Queen whose beauty is like Provence.   To Mary Stuart.

He and BEATON drink.

Mary : Would I were a better toast.

Riccio (*to* MARY BEATON) : You should see the south, mistress.   I hear talk of a love match—the Lord Ogilvy of Boyne it is said.   It would make a sweet honeymoon.

Beaton : I am sure you have a shrewd judgment, Master Riccio.

Mary : Now, David, we will have none of these encouragements.   Must I lose all my friends ?

Riccio : There's an old fellow in Toulouse there who cobbles and makes flutes.   There were never flutes like them.   To hear one is to have the words come pit, pat, and there's a song as soon as you will. Everything there grows like that.   Here it is as though one were under stones, damp, pressed down, all gloom.   But there—ah, but madam, you know.

Beaton : You are glad to go ?

Riccio : It all comes back—how can one help it ? Though it is grief to go from so sweet a service. Even the wine is brighter there.   My papers, madam —shall I deliver them to you ?

Mary : Yes—before you go.   Will you remember Mary Stuart when you hear the cobbler's flute ?

Riccio : I shall remember her always.

Mary : Safely at least I hope, David.

Riccio : But I have no choice in going, madam ?

Mary : None.   Life will be none the more civil for your loss.   I will say that.   Now sing to me for the last time, David.

Riccio (singing) :

> Green shoots we break the morning earth
> > And flourish in the morning's breath;
> We leave the agony of birth
> > And soon are all midway to death.
>
> While yet the summer of her year
> > Brings life her marvels, she can see
> Far off the rising dust, and hear
> > The footfall of her enemy.

> *As he is ending, the handle of the door is turned, and then there is a loud knock.*

Mary : What's that ?

> *The knocking is repeated.* RICCIO *and* BEATON *rise.*

Mary (to BEATON*)* : See what it is.

> BEATON *goes to the door and opens it. Outside is a low murmur of voices.* DARNLEY *comes in.*

Mary : What does this mean ?

Darnley : There are envoys here to speak with the secretary of the Queen.

Mary : They send a strange herald. Do kings turn grooms ?

Darnley : I was coming——

Mary : But we sent word below that we had retired.

Darnley : And so the door was locked. I know. But a husband may be capricious. I found them, asking for the secretary of the Queen. They are waiting.

Mary : Let them come in.

Darnley : It is the secretary.

Riccio : Who are they, my lord ?

Darnley : Who are they?   Shall I go and ask them ?

Riccio : Does Your Grace not know them ?

Darnley : It is dark out there.

Riccio : Shall I go, madam ?

Mary (*to* DARNLEY) : You swear you know nothing of this ?

Darnley : I ?   Swear ?   Oh, yes, I swear.

Mary (*softly*) : No, Riccio, I will go.

She moves across to the door.   Then, loudly—

Go, Riccio.   See what they want.   Your cloak— it's cold beyond.

> *She takes up* RICCIO'S *cloak and throws it round her.*   DARNLEY, *watching her almost in a dreadful hope, creeps away from the door.   She is about to move out when* BEATON *stops her.*

Beaton : Madam, this is wildness.   Either it is nothing, or you take on a danger that you must not.

To DARNLEY.

Why may they not come in here ?

Darnley (*indifferently*) : I know nothing, I tell you. If the Queen wills.

Mary : Very well.   Go, Riccio.

Riccio : Is it safe ?

Beaton : They would not dare, at the Queen's door.

Mary : Go.   There can be nothing to fear.   And we do not govern fate.

> RICCIO *goes out.*   DARNLEY *moves across to the door.   He locks it and takes the key.*

Darnley : The Queen has retired.   Let us talk.

Mary : Why do you lock the door ?

Darnley: I found it so—I thought it was the Queen's will.

> *There is a loud scream outside, and running steps towards the door, which is beaten violently as* RICCIO *tries to enter. Then, a struggle and scream upon scream. Then silence, and footsteps hurrying away.*

Mary (to DARNLEY): Open it!

Darnley: I should have questioned them more closely.

Mary: Open.

> DARNLEY *unlocks and opens the door upon* RICCIO's *body.*

Mary: For shame! A poor simpleton like that.

Darnley: I was in the Queen's chamber. And no one knows. No one in Europe would believe it of the King of Scotland. But I was careless. I should have questioned them more closely.

> *He steps out over* RICCIO's *body and goes.*

Mary (after a pause, looking down at RICCIO): A fantastic nothing. Poor fellow. But the reckoning shall be as though for a great lover. Go, Beaton. Bid them come up. Have the watch summoned. Let him be taken away. This is his poor little tragedy. Ours remains. Go.

> BEATON *goes out.* MARY *closes the door. She goes to the window, and draws back the curtain, filling the room with bright moonlight. She looks out, silent for a few moments, and then sings softly.*

Mary (*singing*) :

> Though brighter wit I had than these,
>> Their cunning brought me down ;
> But Mary's love-story shall please
>> Better than their renown.

> Not Riccio nor Darnley knew,
>> Nor Bothwell, how to find
> This Mary's best magnificence
>> Of the great lover's mind.

The candle gutters out. She throws the window open to the balcony. Voices, as of a dream, are heard from beyond. MARY stands listening.

First Voice : It's a damned silly song. What's it all about . . .

Second Voice : Look at this Queen. She tells you, doesn't she, doesn't she ?

First Voice : What does a dead queen know about me ? You talk nonsense. The moon has your wits, you're like that crazy singer out there. Mary Stuart can tell me nothing I say.

MARY goes along the balcony, out of sight.

My God ! What's that ?

The Voice of Mary : Boy, I can tell you everything.

THE CURTAIN FALLS.

ACT II

*The same room, a year later. It is night-time. MARY
BEATON is reading at the table by candle-light.
Once she goes to the window and listens, then again
from her reading to the door. She returns again to
the book, and after a few moments there is a knock
at the door. She opens it to BOTHWELL, who
comes in.*

Bothwell: Is the Queen here?

Beaton: No, my lord. She is at Kirk o' Fields
with the King.

Bothwell: The King—yes.

Beaton: He is very ill.

Bothwell: Ill—yes.

Beaton: She should be back soon.

Bothwell: I have business. I will return.

Beaton: Shall I tell the Queen?

Bothwell: You are very faithful to the Queen.

Beaton: I can be that at least.

Bothwell: I, too.

Beaton: My lord?

Bothwell: Have you noticed any change in her?
Towards the King I mean? Do not be afraid—I
am safe.

Beaton: She pities him because he ails.

Bothwell: No more?

57

Beaton: I think not.

Bothwell: No fresh affection?

Beaton: That could never be.

Bothwell: She is in danger.

Beaton: Always, I know.

Bothwell: But especially. Now—to-night.

Beaton: She hazards so much. She goes about unattended. It would be so easy. What must I do?

Bothwell: Will you be instructed?

Beaton: Indeed—for her safety.

Bothwell: There is a design against the King.

Beaton: How?

Bothwell: And against the Queen.

Beaton: If you are warned, is it not enough?

Bothwell: You have to help. I have to go very cautiously. I cannot do all. There must be some-one who has the Queen's ear, and then we may be hopeful. You can save the Queen—but you must be exact.

Beaton: I would not fail.

Bothwell: The King is sick. He may die. He lies there without physicians—a slight fever it seems, but these things are sudden. If he were to die it could be small grief anywhere—eh?

Beaton: And yet it is a man's death. I do not think he is so ill as that. The Queen does not think it either.

Bothwell: Listen. These lords have grown ambitious to extremity. The King is in the way. To-night they will work. The King's end is near. And they will seize the Queen or it is their intention. Then everything is to their hand.

Beaton : But this must be told. I must go—the Queen must be told.

> *She moves towards the door.* BOTHWELL
> *stops her.*

Bothwell : That would be useless. Besides, there are eyes everywhere. Nothing will happen to the King until the Queen leaves Kirk o' Fields. She will not be harmed.

Beaton : But what is this—are you one in the design ?

Bothwell : I know of it.

Beaton : But the King—not that—I do not understand.

Bothwell : With or without me, the King's end is fixed. That was inevitable. And I care nothing for the King.

Beaton : But to conspire against him—his death.

Bothwell : It was to be, I tell you. They were resolved, nothing could have shaken them. Not that I had any anxiety to shake their resolution. But I did not devise it—I merely know of it.

Beaton : I care nothing for the King—he has been monstrous. But that. What am I to do ?

Bothwell : You cannot meddle, nor should you.

Beaton : And the Queen ? Are you in that design, too ?

Bothwell : Again, I am informed merely.

Beaton : What will you do ?

Bothwell : Save her.

Beaton : How—to what ?

Bothwell : I love the Queen—and there is no one who can give her more in this starved country than

I, giving her that. You know it—she has said as much to you, her friend—come now?

Beaton: I think——

Bothwell: Yes, yes. You know it. Well, to-night there will be a swift stroke, deadly, up there at Kirk o' Fields. There will be no traces left—all is very cunning. Then they will come here, every foot of the way is prepared and watched, and the Queen will be taken.

Beaton: But if she were warned?

Bothwell: What guard has she? They would be powerless—these lords have worked everywhere. It would mean a little more bloodshed, that is all. They have reckoned against all mishaps.

Beaton: But surely something can be done?

Bothwell: Yes, by us.

Beaton: Tell me.

Bothwell: The lords think I am with them. They are in meeting now; within half an hour I must be there. Presently you will hear disaster—it will be plain. Before they can get here I shall return, and the Queen must leave with me.

Beaton: But you said that every way was watched.

Bothwell: That is it. You must help there.

Beaton: What do you mean?

Bothwell: What is that?

He goes to the door.

I thought I heard her. Quickly then, and mistake nothing. There are two things for you to do. Use her mind to some disaster that is near—say you overheard something—fear that there is conspiracy against her. If she comes before I go, I can say nothing directly of that—she might suspect I knew something about Darnley—that I knew more than was said. She would call her guard, send them out—it would confuse everything and prevent nothing.

Beaton: But is that honest?

Bothwell: Honest—what is honesty to-night? I must get the Queen away I tell you. Darnley is beyond our saving. If not to-night it will be to-morrow or to-morrow. There is devilment every-where. I must take her. Darnley gone, she shall be safe with me. I will defend her, and she shall starve no longer in her heart. To-night it can be done. Play upon her fears—let them work. Tell her that I, and I alone, am her safety if disaster comes. She will listen—her love is ripe for that. You serve her so, never fear. That is your charge in part. And then this. The Close is watched by Colin Bruce. It is our only hope. You have some influence with him?

Beaton: He has said so.

Bothwell: Use it. Let your wits tell you how, but use it. When you hear disaster, as you will, see that Colin keeps the south side of the Close for an hour, leaving the Pine row clear. Can you do that?

Beaton: I will try.

Bothwell: That, or we lose. You shall join us. The Queen can learn all in due time. And do not fail anywhere.

Beaton: I will serve as I can.

Bothwell: Ssh! She is coming.

The door is opened, and MARY STUART *comes
in, cloaked.*

Mary : You ?

Bothwell : I heard you were up there alone. I
feared for your safety.

BEATON *takes* MARY'S *cloak and goes into the
far room.*

Mary : Why should you fear ?   I do not.

Bothwell : But you must.   Danger moves everywhere.

Mary : I am on terms with danger.   I am used
to it.

Bothwell : But for those who love you——

Mary : Those—who are they ?

Bothwell : For me who love you.

Mary : Man, do you love me so well ?

Bothwell : You know it.

Mary : You believe it.

Bothwell (*taking her and kissing her*) : We know it
—don't we—don't we ?

Mary : I told you—it was a year ago, nearly to a
night.   You remember, when Riccio—at that door.
There was but the minute between us, I said.   It
has been for a year—or you have persisted for a
year.   It is much, more than was likely.   It's a
black night—it makes one think of shelter, the
shelter that is found nowhere, for me.

Bothwell : Why do you deny yourself always, thus ?
Why do you not believe my devotion ?   What gain
is there in this refusal and refusal ?   Come away
with me.   Your throne means nothing to you as the
time is—your authority is drained on every side—

you are threatened daily. The lords work against you—England waits the moment that seems to her to be almost here—the certain moment. Leave it all. Come with me.

Mary: No, it cannot be. All would be lost then, irrevocably. There is the King still.

Bothwell: Make me your commander. Give it out that the perils of treason about you make your withdrawal necessary. Let me be known as your soldier. They may believe what they will—it is a story strong enough against misproof. We can wait —we can strike more safely from a distance—you can be the better established for it. Here, who knows what bad chance may fall? It is policy I plead, sound policy—and it gives us our love.

Mary: No—no—there is the King I say.

Bothwell: But he is nothing to you, nothing surely? After all this—Riccio remember, and——

Mary: I need no remembrancers. It is in my heart, all of it. But he is sick, rather pitiful. And for your policy—how if the Queen forsake her husband when he is sick? What will Europe say to that?

Bothwell: What does Europe know of Darnley's sickness, or care?

Mary: It would learn, and there are those who would make caring their business.

Bothwell: Woman, woman, why do you persuade against yourself? You know it is good counsel I give. Your blood knows it. You do not want courage?

Mary: Perhaps.

Bothwell: Take it from me.

Mary: It would be none, so. But I do not think my courage is at fault. Your love could not better me; I fear that.

Bothwell: You want my love, burningly you want it.

Mary: I know—yes. But for an enterprise like this love must be durable. Yours would fail—it is not a fault in you, but it would.

Bothwell: Even so, what then has been lost?

Mary: A shadow merely—a hope, a little hope, I do not know of what—but that out of some fortunate moment, somehow it might come.

Bothwell: What?

Mary: The love that should save me.

Bothwell: But time goes. Danger is here, now. And I love you, now. Your love, your shadow— where is that?

Mary: I know. But in my heart it is all I have left. Nothing, a poor nothing—but all. If I go with you, it is but one step farther into the darkness, the last. Even the shadow would be lost. I am too wise in grief. I am wiser even than my blood. That's lamentable, isn't it? But I have come to that.

Bothwell: If the King were dead?

Mary: How do you mean?

Bothwell: He trails in your thoughts still.

Mary: I tell you no.

Bothwell: Why do you risk the night to see him then?

Mary: Little gusts of compassion, I suppose.

Bothwell: I told you.

Mary: But he is nothing. Do you need to be told that—Darnley, who has been a malady in my life, and even so is I think forgotten.

Bothwell: Mary, I am strong—stronger to-night than you are. If I thought that Darnley—but no I do not think it.

Mary: There is an echo in that.

Bothwell: An echo?

Mary: A year ago, Darnley himself in this room. It was Riccio then.

Bothwell: It is no matter. I tell you that I am for your lover—that nothing can change that—that I am stronger than you. Life here has no meaning for you—it may have disaster. You know that I have reason in my words, and you will not listen. Again, will you dare, now, and greatly? It is security, it is our consummation. Will you come?

Mary: If I should waste all—it might be as good an end as another. But no, no—the chances are too small.

Bothwell (*again taking her in his arms*): Do you not feel that my prayer has authority—my bidding. You are in my arms—you are no queen, you are my subject. If you stay they will destroy your throne—if you stay you will destroy yourself. You have fires. Can you quench them? Mary, my beloved, I am stronger than you. Come. I bid it.

> MARY *stays a moment, bound in his arms.*
> *Then she slowly releases herself.*

Mary: It is magnificent. But I told you. I am wiser than my blood.

Bothwell: Then, listen. I know these lords—they

thrive in every corner about you. Your hours are known to them, and you know hardly the servants in your hall. They may strike here, or there, but it will come. I shall watch. But I am one only. Think of all I have said. Let your blood remember it, too—let it grow wiser—know it for your best wisdom. And when the blow falls I shall be near—look for me. They mistrust me, but my wits are as good as theirs. And when I come again on this errand, it may mean choice at but a minute's rate. And then you will answer as I bid you. Look for me, always. No moment is safe, and I am ready.

He goes.

MARY *makes the least sign of a movement after him, but it is checked immediately. Forlornly she goes to the far door.*

Mary : Beaton.

Beaton : Yes, madam (*entering*). So late and alone. Why will you do it, madam? Not a doorway is safe for you.

Mary : Now, Beaton, not you too. I will not be scolded. I must go to bed.

She goes into the far room. BEATON *arranges a small table, with mirror, comb and brushes, candles in the right place. She is singing Mary's song to herself. After a few moments* MARY *comes back, wearing a long straight gown. She sits at the table, her hair being combed and brushed by* BEATON *as they talk.*

Beaton : How is the King, madam?

Mary : The fever passes. A day or two should mend him.

Beaton : Must you go again ?

Mary : I promised. I owe him nothing, and he cares nothing for me. But sick men are poor creatures. One cannot wholly disregard even a sick Darnley.

Beaton : Is he content at Kirk o' Fields ?

Mary : He asks always to return here. But I will not have that—that at least I am fixed on. Even the people accept that now.

Beaton : One hears so much.

Mary : What have you heard ?

Beaton : It is better that you should not be with the King, I think.

Mary : Yes. But why do you say that now ?

Beaton : There are mutterings — conspiracies I think.

Mary : What do you mean ?

Beaton : These lords would gain all.

Mary : What have you heard, Beaton ? What is it ?

Beaton : I was walking this afternoon. I came on two men at a yard corner. They were talking. I heard a phrase or two. ' Darnley—there's the obstacle,' one said, and the other, ' Yes, if the Queen were moved, it would be nothing with Darnley about still.'

Mary : If the Queen were moved ?

Beaton : That's what he said.

Mary : Who were they ?

Beaton : I do not know. They saw me then, and were gone.

Mary : How moved ?

Beaton : I don't know, madam. But these men

would stay for nothing, I am sure of that.   I have been faithful to you, madam ?

Mary : You only I think, Beaton, my girl.

Beaton : If I might counsel you.

Mary : What can I do ?

Beaton : I love you, madam, but I am nothing. There is only one strong friend about you.

Mary : You mean Bothwell ?

Beaton : You know it too.   I am glad.

Mary : Has he been prompting you ?

Beaton : Only speaking out of his anxiety.

Mary : What would you have ?

Beaton : I would trust all to him.   There is no one else.

Mary : Did he speak of Darnley ?

Beaton : Of Darnley, madam ?

Mary : Of Darnley.

Beaton : I know that he is not loved.

Mary : Did he speak of him ?

Beaton : Something, I think.   But I thought only of his anxiety for you.

Mary : What did he say of Darnley ?

Beaton : Gossip.   Nothing.

Mary : But what was it ?

Beaton : Only of dangers, creeping here and there.

Mary : Be plain.   What was it ?

Beaton : No more than that.   No—that was all.

Mary : So.

Beaton : The King must take his chance.   As we all do here.

Mary : Yes.   As Riccio did.   There was no more ?

Beaton : No, madam.   Do consider my Lord Bothwell. If there should be any sudden extremity I mean.

Mary: He has many advocates. Three of us. It was a year ago, Beaton. Poor fellow, just at the door. How it comes back. And the King's bawdy song—do you remember? He has taken to them since, it is his chief occupation. It was a poor ugly little villainy. Why do I trouble even to visit his sickness? We are strange.

> *There is a light tapping at the door.*

Mary: What is that?

> *The tapping is repeated.*

Mary: See who it is.

> BEATON *opens the door.* DARNLEY *is there, white-faced in a black cloak and hood.*

Mary: What is this?

Darnley: I had to come. I am afraid. When you had gone I grew more afraid. I stole out.

Mary: But this is folly. You are sick. You should be abed.

Darnley: Mary, let me stay here.

Beaton: Madam, you cannot——

Darnley: This woman—who is she—send her away.

Mary: Leave us, Beaton.

Beaton: Your pardon—but I beg you, madam——

Mary: Leave us.

> BEATON *goes.*

Mary: Why do you come? It is madness.

Darnley: I know. But I am afraid I tell you. I am watched. Men were in my steps, things moved in shadows as I came.

Mary: You must go back.

Darnley: For God's sake, Mary, let me stay.

Mary: No.   It is too late for that.

Darnley: What have I done?

Mary: Everything—nothing.

Darnley: I will mend.   I will love you, Mary, love you.

Mary: That is intolerable.

Darnley: I am afraid.

Mary: Why should I bear your fear?

Darnley: I meant nothing.

Mary: You have spared me nothing.

Darnley: You still harp on Riccio.

Mary: No, I have forgotten him.   I remember you.

Darnley: I saw another man out there.   Was it Bothwell?

Mary: Again you begin.

Darnley: Was it Bothwell?

Mary: Can you learn nothing?   Go away.

Darnley: Let me stay.

Mary: No, I tell you, no.

Darnley: What is Bothwell doing?

Mary: Go.

Darnley: Very well then.   I killed Riccio, damn you.

Mary: Go.

Darnley: I killed him out there.   I was here, in the room, here, but I killed him.   Let Bothwell watch—I have experience.   You are a miserable Queen, I'm glad of that.

Mary: Go, I tell you.

Darnley: No, no—let me stay.   I am afraid.

Mary: You are shameless.   Go.

Darnley : But you will come to me again. That at least. I do you little good, you say ; perhaps, but you are strong. You keep fear away.

Mary : I have no anger for you. But expect nothing from me. You make it impossible.

Darnley : I'll go. I would have loved you. But I hate you, I hate well. The dirty Italian learnt it. Bothwell—he's better game, isn't he ? You pretty harlot of Scotland.

> *He goes out, merely a hysteria.* MARY *locks the door, and listens for a moment. She moves away, and at once there is a knocking.*

Mary : Who ?

Darnley (*outside*) : Let me come back. I am afraid I tell you. Mary—Mary.

> MARY *does not answer.*

Let me come in. Harlot — harlot — harlot. I killed Riccio. I told you I would. I'm going.

> *There is silence, while* MARY *sits at the table, her fortitude at breaking point. She regains herself and calls.*

Mary : Beaton.

Beaton (*entering*) : Has he gone ?

Mary : Life is poisoned, all of it, all of it. Barbs, barbs. Beaton, my girl, my girl.

> *She breaks down and sobs in* BEATON'S *arms.*

Beaton : Madam—my darling, my darling. You poor queen—there, there.

> *The strain passes and* MARY *rises.*

Mary : I must sleep. Give it me.

> BEATON *fills a small phial and gives it to her ; she drinks it. As they prepare to go, another knock, sharp and open, comes at the door.*

Beaton (at the door): Who is it?

Randolph (outside): Randolph. Can I speak to Her Majesty? It is urgent.

Mary: Open.

> BEATON *does so, and* RANDOLPH *comes in, carrying a document. He bends to* MARY'S *hand.*

Randolph: Your pardon, madam, for this late intrusion. But messengers from England have arrived in the night. Can I speak with you?

Mary: Be seated.

> BEATON *goes and* MARY *and* RANDOLPH *take their places at the table.*

Mary: You are late.

Randolph: You have been gracious to me, madam. I would be of some service.

Mary: What is it?

Randolph: I do not know who is the informer, but there are bad reports in London.

Mary: Of whom?

Randolph: Of events here.

Mary: Events?

Randolph: Projects, rather.

Mary: How bad reports?

Randolph: I go beyond my duty in coming thus. But I remember.

Mary: What are the reports?

Randolph: It is said that the King's life is threatened.

Mary: Who says it?

Randolph: I am not told.

Mary: Threatened—by whom?

Randolph: It is said that Your Majesty could tell.

Mary: But . . . You do not believe that, Randolph?

Randolph: I do not, madam.

Mary: It's a cunning throw. Very. You know that it is impossible?

Randolph: What, madam?

Mary: That I should . . . Randolph, you know the King is a poor enough thing in my life, you cannot but know it. But not that. Even he could not make me as contemptible as that.

Randolph: I am sure of it. That is why I came.

Mary: What have you to say?

Randolph: There may be a conspiracy against the King. It is not unlikely. If it prospers, it is clear from this (*the paper*) that your name will be spoken.

Mary: What am I to do?

Randolph: We must work and at once. Hours are precious—if it is moving, any moment may be chosen. We must discover the springs. I will help as I can. You must warn Darnley—it is your best defence. I suspect some—Lethington, shall we say, and—you know them. They are very secret, and they have set suspicion towards you.

Mary: I will go to Darnley now, to-night. Can you know that?

Randolph: Indeed, fully.

Mary: You are generous.

Randolph: It is my wish, madam.

Mary: Shall I bring Darnley here?

Randolph: As you think. It would be dangerous, but brave. It might tell.

Mary : Come to me in the morning. Whatever comes, I thank you. It was chivalrous of you.

Randolph : You instructed me, madam.

She gives him her hand and he goes.

Mary : Beaton.

BEATON *comes in.*

Mary : I must go to Kirk o' Fields.

Beaton : Not again to-night, madam.

Mary : Yes, now.

Beaton : But, madam——

Mary : I tell you, now. Ask no questions—there is danger up there, and I must go. My cloak.

Beaton : Madam. I implore——

Mary : Beaton! . . . Bring my cloak.

BEATON *fetches the cloak and helps her mistress.*

Mary : It's a strange errand. An anniversary—in a month it would be a year, Beaton. . . . And now, by the door where he died, to save one by whom he died. It's fantastic living, profitless living. There. I may bring the King with me.

Beaton : Madam, but why? You should not be with the King, not to-night.

Mary : It must be. What do you know, Beaton?

Beaton : Nothing, madam, nothing, but I am afraid.

Mary : You too. Courage seems so simple. Surely we can come to that, at least. You need not wait for me.

Beaton : Madam, if I could but tell you—I do not know——

Mary : Girl, what is it? All the evening——

> *Out of the silence the thunder of a great ex-*
> *plosion is heard, reverberating across the night.*
> MARY *stands fixed in astonishment,* BEATON
> *shaken with fear.*

Mary : What was that ?

Beaton : What was it, madam ?

Mary : Do you know ?

Beaton : Something terrible has happened.

Mary (*throwing the window open*) : It was up there. It was at Kirk o' Fields.

Beaton : It was something terrible.

Mary : What did Bothwell say to you ?

Beaton : Nothing, nothing—it was nothing. What have they done ?

Mary : You are lying.

Beaton : Madam, I love you. I am afraid. I do not know what to do.

Mary (*taking off her cloak*): Find Sir Thomas Randolph. Tell him to come here.

> *She goes, carrying her cloak, into the far room.*
> *As* BEATON *moves to the door it is opened by*
> BOTHWELL.

Bothwell : Where is the Queen ?

Beaton : In there.

Bothwell : To the Close, at once, and do not fail. All depends on that.

Beaton : I am sent to Sir Thomas Randolph.

Bothwell : To the Close, I tell you. No, this way. Go.

> BEATON *goes out by the main door.*

Bothwell : Madam, Mary.

> MARY *comes in.*

Mary : You have come.

Bothwell : Yes.

Mary : What has happened ?

Bothwell : As I foretold. Kirk o' Fields is destroyed.

Mary : Darnley, too ?

Bothwell : Yes.

Mary : And now ?

Bothwell : They are coming here.

Mary : They must come.

Bothwell : They will take you, and what then ? And they have contrived suspicion against you. You must come with me. What better reason ? You have been warned, you know of the treason, you know that it aims at you, too. Escape was your only way. Who can question that ? And I love you, Mary— come. You have no choice. To-morrow you can proclaim me leader of your arms. The present here is destruction. There, in the future, who knows ? We can play strongly. And there is no other way.

Mary (*after a moment's pause*) : Either way, I am snared. But I will go.

BOTHWELL *hurriedly fetches her cloak.*

Bothwell : Quickly ; they will be here. We can get across the Close. I will see. Quickly. A moment only.

> *He goes out by the far door,* MARY *stands at the open window, putting on her cloak.* RANDOLPH *comes in.*

Mary : The summons came too late.

Randolph : The summons ?

Mary : I sent for you.

Randolph : I had no summons.

Mary : It is no matter.

Randolph : You heard—out there ?

Mary : Yes.

Randolph : Was it the King ?

Mary : Yes.

Randolph : Darnley—dead.

Mary : Darnley was nothing. As Riccio was nothing.

Randolph : What will you do ?

Mary : I am going.

Randolph : It is well. With whom ?

Mary : Bothwell.

Randolph : Bothwell ?

Mary : Yes. Bothwell—is nothing.

Randolph : May fortune be with you.

Mary : It will not. We become what we are for ever. How strange. Do you ever dream, Randolph ?

Randolph : Madam, can I do anything ?

Mary : Good-night, Randolph.

He goes.

Mary : We become what we are for ever. We are part of life for ever. It was a year ago. Poor boy —poor boy. If he would but listen. What a thing was that to dream. Mary Stuart can tell me nothing I say. Poor boy.

Bothwell (*from beyond*) : Mary ! . . . Mary !

MARY *does not answer. Then she half turns to the direction of* BOTHWELL'S *voice, and slowly moves towards him.*

THE CURTAIN FALLS.

E. M. Cooper.

November 28th. 1923.